D1523284

INSIDE THE
WORLD CUP

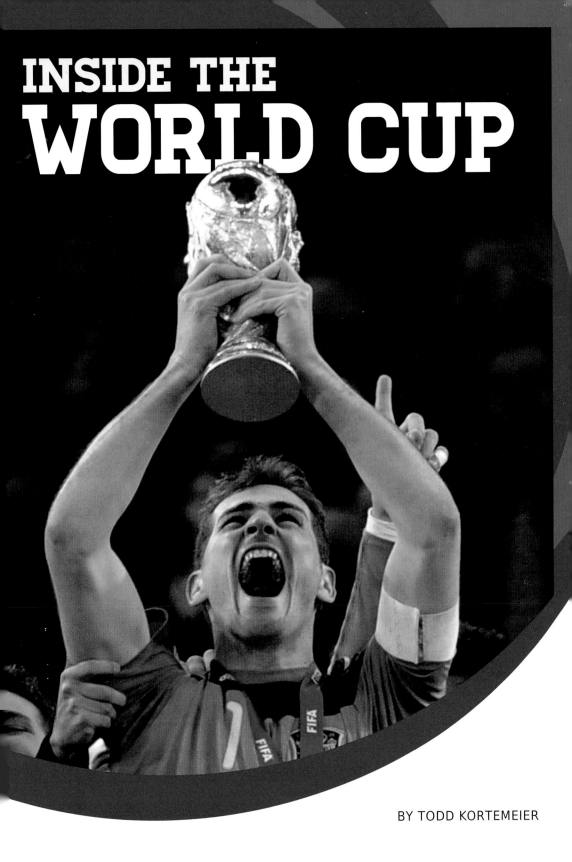

BY TODD KORTEMEIER

Published by The Child's World®
1980 Lookout Drive • Mankato, MN 56003-1705
800-599-READ • www.childsworld.com

Acknowledgments
The Child's World®: Mary Berendes, Publishing Director
Red Line Editorial: Design, editorial direction, and production
Photographs ©: Martin Meissner/AP Images, cover, 1, 26; AP Images, 5; Joshua Paul/
AP Images, 6, 9; Shutterstock Images, 10; Felipe Dana/AP Images, 13; Jon Super/AP
Images, 14; Bill Kostroun/AP Images, 16; Tony Gutierrez/AP Images, 18; VJ Lovero/
SI/Icon Sportswire, 21; Aris Messinis/AP Images, 23; Franck Faugere/DPPI/Icon
Sportswire, 24; Hassan Ammar/AP Images, 27

ISBN 9781634074391

LCCN 2015946281

Printed in the United States of America
Mankato, MN
December, 2015
PA02283

ABOUT THE AUTHOR
Todd Kortemeier is a writer and journalist from Minneapolis.
He is a graduate of the University of Minnesota's School of
Journalism & Mass Communication.

TABLE OF
CONTENTS

FAST FACTS

What is it? The World Cup is a 32-team soccer tournament played every four years. Teams representing countries from all over the globe compete.

How do they qualify? Teams complete a series of regional qualifying tournaments to see who plays in the World Cup. More than 200 teams try to make it.

What do they play for? The current World Cup Trophy was first awarded in 1974. It replaced the original Jules Rimet Trophy, which had been stolen. The current model is 14.5 inches (36.8 cm) tall. It weighs 13.61 pounds (6.18 kg). The trophy is made of 18-karat gold. Winning countries get their name inscribed on it.

When is it? The tournament is usually played over several weeks in summer. However, the 2022 World Cup in Qatar is scheduled to be different. It will be played in November and December because summers in Qatar are too hot.

Where is it? Any Fédération Internationale de Football Association (FIFA) member nation may bid to host the World Cup. FIFA is the governing body of world soccer. A group of FIFA representatives votes to decide on a host nation.

When was the first one? Uruguay hosted the first World Cup in 1930. Thirteen countries competed for the title, with the host country winning it all.

How many people go? The 2014 World Cup in Brazil attracted 3,429,873 fans. It was the second-highest turnout ever. The 1994 tournament in the United States drew 3,587,538 fans.

How many people watch? The World Cup is one of the most-watched events in the world. In 2010, 909 million people watched the final match. More than 1 billion viewers are estimated to have watched in 2014.

Chapter 1

A TEAM'S PERSPECTIVE: TIMOR-LESTE

I t was a hot night in Dili, Timor-Leste, on March 12, 2015. That is when the country's World Cup qualifying matches began. The tournament itself would not kick off in Russia for another three years. But the dream had already started for the Timorese. Their players had to take off work for the match. Timor-Leste had few **professionals**.

Timor-Leste was one of 208 countries attempting to qualify for the World Cup. The Southeast Asian nation was one of the newest members of FIFA. Timor-Leste was making its third attempt to participate in the tournament. It had never won a qualifying match. Dili's National Stadium had just 10,000 seats. Each one was filled as Timor-Leste took on Mongolia. More fans watched the game on a giant TV screen outside the gates.

◀ **Timor-Leste celebrates a goal in a qualifying match against Malaysia on June 11, 2015.**

"Timorese players are very passionate for [soccer]," former team captain Alfredo Esteves said. "If you go around the streets of Dili, you will see a lot of kids kicking a ball, even without shoes."[1]

Teams qualify for the World Cup by doing well in regional matches. Timor-Leste is an island located between Indonesia and Australia. The Timor-Leste team played against other teams from that area. If the team survived the first round, it went to the next stage. That is when the region's top teams joined the qualifying process. The Timorese would have to beat teams such as Japan and Australia. They had players from some of the world's best **club** teams.

But the Timorese were not worrying about that yet.

"It doesn't matter if Timor win[s], or Mongolia win[s], the most important thing is that [soccer] wins," Francisco Lay, president of the country's soccer association, said.[2]

But the Timorese definitely wanted to win. They started fast. Chiquito "Quito" Filipe do Carmo put the home side up 1–0 in the fourth minute. Then he struck again in the seventh. Timor-Leste stretched the lead to 4–0. The match finished 4–1.

But Timor-Leste had not yet advanced. The team had to beat Mongolia in a two-game series. The second match was in Mongolia. It was cold there. It would be quite different from Dili.

▲ Timor-Leste hoped to make history by qualifying for the 2018 World Cup in Russia.

In the second game, Timor-Leste scored another early goal and held on to win 1–0. Timor-Leste had made the second round. Things would get much harder with better Asian teams joining. But with its first two World Cup qualifying victories, Timor-Leste had already made history.

Chapter 2

A COUNTRY'S PERSPECTIVE: PELADA PLAYERS OF BRAZIL

Sixteen-year-old Lucas Daniel woke up after only a few hours of sleep. He had stayed up until 5:30 a.m. playing soccer. Now he was headed out to play again. Up to that morning, Lucas believed he had played every day of his life. The game was a national obsession. Lucas once dislocated a toe while he was playing. But the game did not stop. In Brazil, it never does.

"I pushed it back into place," Lucas said. "And then I kept playing."[3]

Almost all Lucas and his friends did was play. Their game was called *pelada*. *Futebol* means "soccer" in Portuguese, the national language of Brazil. But futebol was something else. Futebol was what they played at the World Cup, hosted by Brazil in 2014. Futebol had real grass fields and big stadiums. Millions of people watched around the world.

◄ **Forward Neymar is one of the brightest stars of Brazil's soccer team.**

Pelada was played on streets, in alleys, and in courtyards. The ball sometimes was not even a ball at all. Players used what they had. They made balls out of cardboard or socks stuffed with paper. Sometimes the balls were not even round.

Lucas and his cousin Diego waited for the next game to start. Another one was always just minutes away.

"We just play whenever," Diego said.

"Remember the kid who played so much we called him Neymar?" Lucas said.

"What happened to him?"

"I don't know. He was scouted by a big team. I don't see him anymore," Lucas said.[4]

That was the dream. The boys hoped pelada would one day lead them to a World Cup stadium. Brazil national team **forward** Neymar started that way. So did Pelé, Ronaldo, and other legendary Brazilian players. It was not an impossible dream. Thousands of Brazilians played professional soccer in leagues around the world.

The dream was not just for boys. Women's soccer in Brazil was still developing. There was no national league. But the country had quality players. Marta was named World Player of the Year five times. She played in foreign leagues. Fourteen-year-old Clara Chaves hoped women's soccer would be taken seriously in Brazil some day. She played for a women's club team. And she held her own on the pelada court.

A major key to Brazil's success was on display in the streets every day. At another pelada game in Rio de Janeiro, Anesio Cornelo watched his son Robson play.

"I think this is good for Brazilian players," Cornelo said. "They play this way, on the court. They learn how to touch the ball, how to control the ball. It is a lot faster here than on a field. They become more skilled than if they just played on grass."[5]

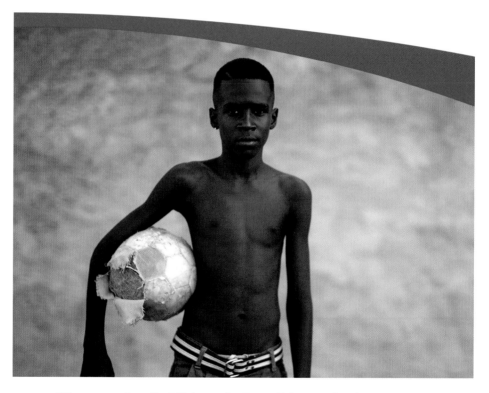

▲ **Thousands of children in Brazil love playing soccer no matter the conditions.**

Chapter 3

THE FANS' PERSPECTIVE: REPUBLIC OF IRELAND FANS

Fans were excited when the Republic of Ireland qualified for the 1990 World Cup in Italy. It was the team's first World Cup. Fans followed the team to Italy. There, they made friends, sang songs, and cheered on their team. The supporters did not expect Ireland to reach the second round. But the team made it to the final 16. Irish supporters had a choice to make.

Many had plans to return to Ireland after the the team's first three games. The fans had jobs and families back home. But the choice was easy for many of them. They stayed with their team.

Even more Irish fans went to the United States for the 1994 World Cup. Only half of the approximately 12,000 traveling fans had tickets. The rest came just to be a part of it all.

◄ Republic of Ireland soccer fans showed their loyalty by traveling all over the world to support their team.

▲ **Ireland midfielder Ray Houghton (8) celebrates after scoring against Italy in the 1994 World Cup.**

"We could do with 100,000 tickets because of the people outside Ireland," Joe Delaney of the Football Association of Ireland said.[6]

There were many people of Irish descent living in the United States. So the Irish team had many supporters. There were loud songs and the green, white, and orange flag of Ireland wherever they went. Some nations' fans were unruly. But the Irish took pride in sportsmanship. Several years earlier, the team had played a match in Luxembourg. Local police expected trouble and brought in extra officers. But they soon learned the Irish were no trouble at all. After the 1990 World Cup, more Italian tourists started visiting Ireland.

"It's all due to the good will of the supporters," Republic of Ireland fullback Kevin Moran said. "We're as proud of them off the pitch as they're proud of us on it."[7]

Ireland's first 1994 World Cup game was against Italy. It was a familiar foe. Italy had knocked Ireland out of the previous World Cup. This match was in New Jersey. There were thousands of Irish fans in the crowd.

"We'd been told the crowd would be two-thirds Italians but, when we walked out, it was the other way round," Republic of Ireland midfielder Ray Houghton said. "Our support was quite incredible."[8] Houghton put the Irish up 1–0 just 11 minutes into the match.

"What followed was beyond pandemonium: 37,000 Irish fans bellowed their delight . . . I've never heard such a noise," Irish fan Danny Kelly later wrote for *The Guardian* newspaper.[9]

The Irish team again made it to the second round. But it met a similar fate. It lost to the Netherlands 2–0. Houghton felt the team was tired. The match was also played in hot conditions in Orlando, Florida. Irish players were not used to playing in the heat. Any World Cup loss is hard. But the Irish fans were still proud. As the players left Orlando, the fans cheered for them. About 250,000 more waited to welcome the team back to Ireland.

Chapter 4

A COACH'S PERSPECTIVE: THE U.S.A.'S BRUCE ARENA

oach Bruce Arena was at the top of American soccer in March 1998. He had just won his second Major League Soccer title with D.C. United. Before that, he had won five college championships with the University of Virginia. Some wondered if he could lead the national team. But he did not expect it to happen.

"I haven't thought about it much," Arena said at the time. "I've got my own job to worry about."[10]

The United States was at the bottom of the soccer world in October 1998. The team finished dead last at that year's World Cup. The United States called on Arena to take over. Results improved. But Arena was not expecting much heading into the 2002 World Cup hosted by South Korea and Japan.

"We're not going to win [the World Cup] because we're not a good enough team," he said. "I don't think anyone is going

◄ U.S. coach Bruce Arena celebrates after his team scores against Mexico at the 2002 World Cup.

to be damaged by us saying that. I mean, how many countries have won it? If we can get a point in the first game, it will put the whole group in chaos."[11]

The United States did more than that. It **upset** Portugal 3–2 in its first game. Portugal was one of the best teams in the world. Nobody expected the Americans to win. Arena's own expectations were low. But he gave his players the confidence they needed.

"Bruce made us feel like we could win," U.S. defender Frankie Hejduk said. "So we were like, we're going to punk these guys, and before you knew it we were up 3–0."[12]

The United States tied its next match. Then it lost to Poland. The loss did not matter. The Americans had done enough to move on to the next round. Their next match was against rival Mexico. The teams knew each other well. They had played in the same **confederation** during qualifying. So Arena changed up the U.S. game plan.

The team surprised its rivals with a different **formation**. The change worked. The United States won 2–0 to move on to the quarterfinal round. The team had not advanced that far since 1930. But there was still work to do.

U.S. defender Frankie Hejduk said Arena instilled belief in the ▶ team before its game against Portugal.

"We're not pretending to be at the same level as the established teams, but the gap has closed considerably," Arena said.[13]

The next match was against Germany. The Germans had won three World Cups. The United States almost pulled off another upset. Germany midfielder Torsten Frings appeared to stop the ball with his hand on the goal line in the 49th minute. But there was no call. If a penalty kick had been awarded, the Americans might have tied the game 1–1.

"If we had gotten the call, there was a good chance we could have won that game," Arena said.[14]

The United States lost 1–0. The World Cup ride was over. But Arena was quick to remind his players what they had done. In four years they had gone from finishing last to reaching the quarterfinals of the World Cup. As players took off their gear, Arena summed it all up for them.

"You showed the world you could play," he said.[15]

Arena was upset Germany midfielder Torsten Frings (22) was ▶ not called for a hand ball in the 49th minute.

Chapter 5

A PLAYER'S PERSPECTIVE: SPAIN'S ANDRÉS INIESTA

Spain midfielder Andrés Iniesta needed just a little bit of space. The 2010 World Cup final between Spain and the Netherlands was a physical game. Fourteen **yellow cards** were issued. That was eight more than the previous record. There was also a red card. The Netherlands tried to disrupt the passing and skill of Iniesta and his teammates. Neither team could take control.

The game was deep into **extra time** with no score. Players on both teams were tired after playing nearly 116 minutes. Only about four minutes were left before penalty kicks. Spain defender Carles Puyol won the ball near his team's goal. Spain steadily built its attack. The team was known for a style of play called *tiki-taka* or "tippy tap." It kept possession of the ball and used quick, precise passing.

◀ Spain midfielder Andrés Iniesta celebrates after winning the 2010 World Cup.

Iniesta got the ball near midfield. He was quickly surrounded. He back-heel passed to a teammate. Then he started running toward the goal. Iniesta ran between two defenders and saw only grass between him and the goal. Spain forward Fernando Torres's pass was blocked. But Spain midfielder Cesc Fàbregas gained possession. He fired a pass into the **goalkeeper's box**.

Iniesta collected the ball with his right foot. He had only goalkeeper Maarten Stekelenburg to beat. Iniesta struck the ball as it bounced. It rocketed toward the far corner of the goal. Stekelenburg got a hand on it. But it was not enough. Spain went up 1–0 with just minutes to play.

Iniesta stretched his arms out wide and ran to the sideline to celebrate. He took off his jersey to reveal a shirt with a message that translated to "Dani Jarque always with us." Jarque was a friend and former teammate who had passed away the year before.

The entire Spanish team ran over and mobbed Iniesta. Soon the final minute ran off the clock. It was official. Spain was the world champion for the first time.

It was yet another big moment for the midfielder. In 2009, Iniesta had scored a late game-winning goal for club team

Iniesta honored former teammate and friend Dani Jarque after ▶ scoring the winning goal.

Barcelona in a Champions League semifinal. That goal inspired a sportswriter to state, "Now we know who the god of football is . . . His name is Andrés."[16]

"I can't quite believe it yet," Iniesta said after the World Cup. "I simply made a small contribution in a game that was very tough, very rough."[17]

As Iniesta answered questions after the game, a gold medal draped around his neck, some familiar faces arrived. Puyol, Fàbregas, and Spain defender Gerard Piqué interrupted the press conference. They were singing and cheering.

"We love you, Andrés," they said in Spanish. "We're the world champions!"[18]

Iniesta celebrates with teammates after scoring the ▶ World Cup-winning goal.

GLOSSARY

club (kluhb): A person plays on a club team when not with the national team. Andrés Iniesta played for the Barcelona club team.

confederation (con-FED-uhr-EH-shun): A confederation is a regional group of teams that compete against each other to qualify for major tournaments. Mexico and the United States play in the same confederation when trying to make it to the World Cup.

extra time (ECKS-truh tym): Extra time is played if a match is tied at the end of regulation time. The 2010 World Cup final went into extra time after it was tied 0–0 at the end of regulation.

formation (fore-MAY-shun): A team's formation is its plan for where players are on the field. The United States used a new formation against Mexico.

forward (FORE-wird): A forward plays primarily in the offensive zone and tries to score goals. Neymar is a forward for Brazil.

goalkeeper's box (GOHL-kee-per-z bahcks): The goalkeeper's box is the area outlined around the goal in which goalkeepers can use their hands. Cesc Fàbregas fired a pass into the goalkeeper's box to Andrés Iniesta.

professionals (pro-FESH-in-uhls): Professionals are players who are paid to play. Timor-Leste did not have many professionals on its team.

upset (UP-set): A team completes an upset when it beats a team it is projected to lose to. The United States upset Portugal in the 2002 World Cup.

yellow cards (YELL-owe kard-z): Yellow cards are shown by referees to players who commit hard fouls. The referee showed 14 yellow cards in the 2010 World Cup final.

SOURCE NOTES

1-2. "Long Road to Russia Begins in Dili." *FIFA*. FIFA. 11 Mar. 2015. Web. 6 Apr. 2015.

3-5. Sam Borden. "Pickup Soccer in Brazil Has an Allure All Its Own." *New York Times*. The New York Times Company. 18 Oct. 2013. Web. 16 Apr. 2015.

6-7. Alexander Wolff. "Here Come the Lads." *Sports Illustrated*. Time Inc. 13 Jun. 1994. Web. 16 Apr. 2015.

8. Chris Bevan. "The Story of the 1994 World Cup." *BBC*. BBC News. 27 May 2010. Web. 16 Apr. 2015.

9. Danny Kelly. "Ireland Invades New York." *The Guardian*. Guardian News and Media Limited. 20 May 2009. Web. 16 Apr. 2015.

10. Grant Wahl. "Amazingly Graceless." *Sports Illustrated*. Time Inc. 23 Mar. 1998. Web. 16 Apr. 2015.

11. Ed Farnsworth. "Looking Back at the U.S. Soccer Team's Historic 2002 World Cup." *Philly.com*. Philadelphia Media Network. 9 May 2014. Web. 16 Apr. 2015.

12. Grant Wahl. "Taking on the World." *Sports Illustrated*. Time Inc. 1 May 2006. Web. 16 Apr. 2015.

13. Ed Farnsworth. 9 May 2014.

14. Grant Wahl. 1 May 2006.

15. Paul Henricksen. "USA vs. Germany 2002 World Cup Highlights." Online video clip. *YouTube*. Google. 10 Apr. 2008. Web. 24 Apr. 2015.

16. Richard Deitsch. "Andrés Iniesta." *Sports Illustrated*. Time Inc. 16 Jun. 2011. Web. 16 Apr. 2015.

17-18. Grant Wahl. "The Agony and the Ecstasy." *Sports Illustrated*. Time Inc. 19 Jul. 2010. Web. 16 Apr. 2015.

TO LEARN MORE

Books

Christopher, Matt. *World Cup*. New York: Little, Brown, and Co., 2010.

Crouch, Terry, and James Corbett. *The World Cup: The Complete History*. London: deCoubertin Books, 2014.

Jökulsson, Illugi. *Stars of the World Cup*. New York: Abbeville Kids, 2014.

Web Sites

Visit our Web site for links about the World Cup: childsworld.com/links

Note to Parents, Teachers, and Librarians: We routinely verify our Web links to make sure they are safe and active sites. So encourage your readers to check them out!

INDEX